how2become

Police Officer Core Competency Keywords, Phrases and Sentences

Example keywords, phrases and sentences to help match the UK police officer core competencies

By Richard McMunn

www.How2Become.com

Orders: Please contact How2Become Ltd, Suite 1, 60 Churchill Square Business Centre, Kings Hill, Kent ME19 4YU.

You can order through Amazon.co.uk under ISBN 9781912370702, via the website www.How2Become.com or through Gardners.com.

You can also order via the e mail address info@how2become.com

ISBN: 9781912370702

First published 2019

Copyright © 2019 How2Become Limited. All rights reserved.

All rights reserved. Apart from any permitted use under UK copyright law, no part of this publication may be reproduced or transmitted in any form or by any means, electronic or mechanical, including photocopying, recording, or any information, storage or retrieval system, without permission in writing from the publisher or under licence from the Copyright Licensing Agency Limited. Further details of such licenses (for reprographic reproduction) may be obtained from the Copyright Licensing Agency Ltd, Saffron House, 6-10 Kirby Street, London EC1N 8TS.

Disclaimer

Please note that the phrases and wording used within this book are to be used for practice purposes only. How2Become.com is not affiliated with any police force, and all guidance and advice provided is designed to help you prepare and practice for the police assessment process. You will need to use your own answers during the selection process, based on your own experiences.

Every effort has been made to ensure that the information contained within this guide is accurate at the time of publication. How2Become Ltd is not responsible for anyone failing any part of any selection process as a result of the information contained within this guide. How2Become Ltd and their authors cannot accept any responsibility for any errors or omissions within this guide, however caused. No responsibility for loss or damage occasioned by any person acting, or refraining from action, as a result of the material in this publication can be accepted by How2Become Ltd.

The information within this guide does not represent the views of any third-party service or organisation.

Attend a 1 Day Police Officer Training Course by visiting:

www.PoliceCourse.co.uk

Get more products for passing any selection process at:

www.How2Become.com

CONTENTS

Introduction by Richard McMunn 7

Competency #1 Public Service 11

Competency #2 Openness To Change 21

Competency #3 Service Delivery 29

Competency #4 Professionalism 35

Competency #5 Decision Making 43

Competency #6 Working With Others 49

Sample Application Form Question & Answer (Competencies 1-6) 57

New Police Officer Core Competencies 63

Competency #7 Emotionally Aware 65

Competency #8 Taking Ownership 69

Competency #9 Working Collaboratively 73

Competency #10 Analyse Critically 77

Competency #11 Deliver, Support & Inspire 81

Competency #12 Innovative And Open Minded 85

Sample Application Form Question & Answer (Competencies 7-12) 89

Sample Assessment Centre Interview Question And Answer 91

A Few Final Words 95

Introduction by Richard McMunn

8 Police Officer Core Competency Keywords, Phrases and Sentences

INTRODUCTION

Over the years, many people have contacted me asking for advice on how to pass the police officer selection process. In an increasingly competitive environment, candidates want to not only develop their skills and understanding of what it takes to pass the police officer selection process, but what they need to do in order to beat the competition. In response to the numerous requests I have received over the years, I decided to put together this guide, which is a collection of keywords, phrases and sentences that, in my opinion, are a close match for the core competencies you will be assessed under.

I want to make it clear from the outset that the keywords, phrases and sentences included within this guide are not guaranteed to get you the scores required to pass, far from it. Instead, they are designed to give you an understanding of how what you write, what you say and what you do during the police officer selection process, can dramatically increase your chances of success.

When using this guide, try to gain an understanding of how each keyword, phrase and sentence is a close match to the specific element of the core competency being assessed. For example, as part of the core competency PUBLIC SERVICE, you will be required to:

Demonstrate a real belief in public service, focusing on what matters to the public and will best serve their interests.

In order to demonstrate this part of the core competency, it is my advice to try and match it with keywords, phrases and sentences during each stage of the selection process. So, if you were answering a specific application form question, or responding to an interview question that assesses the core competency of PUBLIC SERVICE, you might write or say any of the following:

- I felt it was important to go out of my way to provide a great service for the customer/client.

- The only way I would be able to meet the needs of the individual was to provide them with outstanding service.

- At all times I felt it was important to focus on what the person needed.

- After gathering the relevant information, I had a thorough understanding of what the person needed.

If you are attending the role play scenarios, you may say any of the following to attempt to match that particular element of the PUBLIC SERVICE core competency:

- "I genuinely want to provide you with the right level of service and I will take responsibility to ensure that happens."

- "In order for me to provide you with the right level of service, I would like to ask you some questions."

- "I need to gather further information which will then enable me to put a plan together to meet your needs."

- "Can you tell me what matters to you in this situation, please?"

The important thing to remember is this: throughout the selection process you are being assessed against the core competencies of a police officer. On that basis, you have to show the assessors that you have the previous experience and the ability to perform the role to the required high standards. The only way you can do this successfully, in my opinion, is to provide the assessors with evidence throughout. What you write, what you say and how you act throughout the selection process is very important. Remember, the assessors do not know you either personally or professionally, and therefore it is your job to make their life as easy as possible when they are marking and assessing you. This guide aims to help you achieve that goal.

Finally, if you would like any further help with preparing effectively for the police officer selection process, we offer a wide range of books, online courses and training days at the website How2Become.com. Please do check them out, as many people are gaining success by using them.

All the best,

Richard McMunn

Attend a one-day police officer training course:

www.PoliceCourse.co.uk

Attend a police officer assessment centre course:

www.PoliceAssessmentCourse.co.uk

Competency #1
Public Service

12 Police Officer Core Competency Keywords, Phrases and Sentences

PUBLIC SERVICE

The first core competency we will take a look at is that of PUBLIC SERVICE. As a police officer, you will have to deliver outstanding service to the public at all times. Not only that, you will also have to show you can meet the ever-changing needs and expectations of the public and understand how your actions impact on the public's perception of you and the police service. Here's what you'll be required to demonstrate not only during the selection process, but also once you become a police officer:

> Demonstrates a real belief in public service, focusing on what matters to the public and will best serve their interests. Understands the expectations, changing needs and concerns of different communities, and strives to address them. Builds public confidence by talking with people in local communities to explore their viewpoints and break down barriers between them and the police. Understands the impact and benefits of policing for different communities, and identifies the best way to deliver services to them. Works in partnership with other agencies to deliver the best possible overall service to the public.

Let's now take a look at my suggested keywords, phrases and sentences for the core competency of PUBLIC SERVICE.

APPLICATION FORM AND INTERVIEWS

Demonstrates a real belief in public service, focusing on what matters to the public and will best serve their interests.

- I felt it was important to go out of my way to provide a great service for the customer/client.

- I wanted to really get to the bottom of the customer's complaint, to find a way to make things better for them.

- I understood that, if my employer's business was to thrive in the future, I would need to provide exceptional service at all times.

- The only way I would be able to meet the needs of the individual was to provide them with outstanding service.

- I focused on the client's needs at all times, as I knew this would be the only way I could deliver the right level of service.

- I asked the person a number of questions to find out what it was exactly they needed from me.

- At all times I felt it was important to focus on what the person needed.

- After gathering the relevant information, I had a thorough understanding of what the person needed.

- I understood that, if I was going to serve their interests I would need to first of all gather more information and find out more about what they needed.

- At every stage of the process, I kept in close contact with the customer/client to ensure I was meeting their needs.

- I am someone who understands how important it is to provide a high level of service to the public, and I can be relied upon to consistently deliver this important value of the police service.

14 Police Officer Core Competency Keywords, Phrases and Sentences

Understands the expectations, changing needs and concerns of different communities, and strives to address them.

- From the information I was getting, it was clear I would need to utilise a diverse set of skills in order to meet their expectations.

- Before I set to work on the project, I spoke to the client on the telephone to get a thorough understanding of their needs.

- After carefully considering my options, I felt the most appropriate way to deal with the situation would be to address their concerns.

- Once I had asked probing questions, I was then able to make the right decision, which would lead to a successful resolution of the problem.

- I listened to the person carefully before making a plan of action that would address their needs and also meet their expectations.

- During the project, the client got in touch with me to request some important changes. I listened carefully to the changes and then worked hard to implement them effectively.

- The police service is an organisation which must respond to the needs of the community it serves. I am someone who is positive about delivering high levels of service and I feel I can consistently meet the expectations of this highly responsible role.

Competency #1 Public Service

Builds public confidence by talking with people in local communities to explore their viewpoints and break down barriers between them and the police.

- I decided to break down the barriers between the two individuals, by asking them questions about how they both felt.
- I could detect conflict between two members of the team, and so I decided to take action to resolve the issue quickly to ensure it didn't impact on the team performance as a whole.
- I asked my manager for her opinion on how I should tackle the project. I was keen to get her viewpoint, as she had lots of experience in this field.
- I felt the only way I would achieve the desired outcome would be to ask the person for their view on how things were going.
- It was important for me to build a positive relationship with the individual.
- I felt I could only gain the person's trust by asking them questions about how they felt and what I could do specifically to solve the problem.
- Although I was confident in my own abilities, I wanted to get my colleague's viewpoint on how he thought I should complete the task.
- During the team task, I asked the other members of the team for their viewpoint on one particular aspect of the project. I felt it was important to obtain a diverse view and opinion of how I should complete the task.

16 Police Officer Core Competency Keywords, Phrases and Sentences

Understands the impact and benefits of policing for different communities, and identifies the best way to deliver services to them.

- I wanted to deliver the best possible service for the individual concerned, and the only way I would achieve this would be to consider the impact of my actions.

- I spent a lot of time focusing on their needs. I knew if I did this, it would allow me to build a positive working relationship moving forward.

- Before commencing work on the task, I considered my options carefully, as I wanted to make sure the service I was providing was the best it could be.

- I thought carefully as to how my actions would impact on the needs of the customer. This approach has served me well in the past, as it allows me to ensure I reach the end result positively.

- I needed to take into consideration everyone's needs and viewpoints. If I didn't do this, I would not be able to provide them with the right level of service.

- I thought carefully about the customer's needs and requirements, before working hard to deliver the service to the standard required.

Works in partnership with other agencies to deliver the best possible overall service to the public.

- I decided to get other people involved, as this would allow me to deliver the right results for the company.

- I knew that the only way I could provide the right level of service would be to involve other departments within our organisation.

- I worked closely with the other members of the team to ensure the task was completed on time and to the required standards.

- I wanted to provide the best possible service to the customer, and so I decided to collaborate with other departments, as they had key strengths in other important areas.

- By working in collaboration with other people, it would allow me to provide the right level of service.

- My end goal was to see to their needs quickly, and the only way I could achieve this was by asking other people for their help and assistance.

- I worked closely with my work colleague to ensure we delivered the right level of service for the customer.

- In order to resolve the customer's complaint, I contacted an external agency to ask them if they would be able to deliver the package faster than our usual courier.

- I am someone who can work in collaboration with other people to deliver the highest possible service standards attainable.

18 Police Officer Core Competency Keywords, Phrases and Sentences

ROLE PLAYS

Demonstrates a real belief in public service, focusing on what matters to the public and will best serve their interests.

- I genuinely want to provide you with the right level of service and I will take responsibility to ensure that happens.

- In order for me to provide you with the right level of service, I would like to ask you some questions.

- I need to gather further information which will then enable me to put a plan together to meet your needs.

- Can you tell me what matters to you in this situation, please?

- I would very much like to resolve this complaint quickly for you. Before I decide on the appropriate course of action, can you tell me how the situation has impacted on you?

- I can see you are very upset about what has just happened to you. In order to help me resolve this situation quickly and effectively, can you explain to me exactly what has happened?

- As the Customer Service Officer, I am here to assist you and provide an exceptional level of service. Before I come up with a plan of action, I would like to ask you some questions.

Competency #1 Public Service

Understands the expectations, changing needs and concerns of different communities, and strives to address them.

- I can totally understand your expectations and I will do all I can to make sure these are met.

- I will now go away and address your concerns, and keep you updated on progress.

- In order to resolve this situation for you, I would like to ask you some probing questions.

- Now that I have had the time to listen to your concerns, I will put a plan of action in place to address these. My plan of action is XYZ.

- Yes, I can totally understand how this situation has made you feel. However, the centre's policy states XYZ, and on that basis I must follow the rules in order to provide our visitors with the correct level of service.

- The guidelines at the centre are here to protect all members of the public and I must ensure there are adhered to.

Builds public confidence by talking with people in local communities to explore their viewpoints and break down barriers between them and the police.

- Please tell me how you feel?

- Can you explain exactly what has just happened to you? I will take notes and then decide on an appropriate course of action.

- I am here to serve you and it is my intention to get your view on how things could be improved.

- I have a plan in place which will help me to build a positive relationship with you.

- I can understand how this must have made you feel. In order to resolve the issue, here's what I plan to do.

- I can assure you I will resolve this situation quickly and efficiently. To achieve this, I will first of all ask you a series of questions.

Understands the impact and benefits of policing for different communities, and identifies the best way to deliver services to them.

- I can now see how the impact of that person's actions has had an effect on you.
- I have had the time to review all of the information available to me and I now have a plan in place to resolve the issue.
- The best way to provide you with the level of service you deserve is XYZ.
- I believe the following course of action will be of benefit to your situation. Here's what I plan to do.
- There is a benefit to the centre's guidelines and code of ethics. If we did not have these, our visitors would not feel safe whilst shopping.
- Whilst I can understand your frustrations, sir, the rules of the centre are here to protect everyone and I must ask you to abide by them.

Works in partnership with other agencies to deliver the best possible overall service to the public.

- In order for me to resolve this situation quickly, I will need to ask XYZ to help me.
- I think the fastest way for me to solve this problem is to involve other work colleagues from here at the centre.
- I will now speak with the other agencies and departments within the centre and ask them to help me resolve the situation in the fastest time possible.

Competency #2
Openness To Change

OPENNESS TO CHANGE

Being open to, and embracing change, are qualities any employer would want in a prospective candidate. In the police service, these qualities are even more important. The police service has to change continually if it is to deliver the service the public expects. Society is changing at a rapid rate, and public services must continually improve and develop. From my own experience of working in the public sector, some employees do not like change. In fact, some of them will attempt to block it by complaining and moaning with phrases such as, "If it isn't broke, why fix it?" This attitude is not helpful. In order to succeed as a police officer in the modern world, you will need to be positive about change and, more importantly, embrace it.

Here's what you'll be required to demonstrate not only during the selection process, but also once you become a police officer:

> Positive about change, adapting rapidly to different ways of working and putting effort into making them work. Flexible and open to alternative approaches to solving problems. Finds better, more cost-effective ways to do things, making suggestions for change. Takes an innovative and creative approach to solving problems.

Let's now take a look at my suggested keywords, phrases and sentences for the core competency of OPENNESS TO CHANGE.

APPLICATION FORM AND INTERVIEWS

Positive about change, adapting rapidly to different ways of working and putting effort into making them work.

- I realised there was a need for change and I was keen to embrace it.

- My manager sought volunteers for the new way of working, and I decided to take these on-board with a positive mindset and attitude.

- I am aware that the only way positive improvement can be achieved is through continual change and development.

- Whilst others in the office viewed the change with trepidation, I decided to embrace it positively and enthusiastically.

- I quickly embraced the proposed changes and worked hard to implement the new way of working.

- I felt positive about the changes being brought in by senior managers and sought ways to embrace said changes.

- Once the new changes to our working practices had been decided, I set about learning the methods and implemented them into my working day as quickly as possible.

- I am excited to have the opportunity to work within an organisation that embraces change positively. I see change as an important factor in continuous development, and always seek to learn and develop new skills periodically, whilst following feedback from my senior managers.

Flexible and open to alternative approaches to solving problems.

- I was very much open to the alternative way of working, as I felt there could be a better way of resolving the situation.

- Another member of the team decided to put forward a fresh way of working. I thought this was a positive contribution and so I decided to embrace it.

- I felt that the only way a positive outcome could be achieved was to try the different method of working.

- The problem needed to be solved quickly, and I encouraged everyone to come up with new and innovative ways of working.

- I was flexible in my approach to the task. By being flexible, the project had every opportunity to succeed.

- I am someone who will always seek better ways of working, whilst learning from each experience in the process.

Finds better, more cost-effective ways to do things, making suggestions for change.

- I felt the current way of working was too expensive, and so I decided to look for ways to make things more cost effective for the organisation.

- During the team meeting, I offered a new and fresh way of working that would hopefully be of benefit to the organisation.

- I volunteered to be the one that would take on the extra workload, as I felt this would help the company save money in the long run.

- Whilst trying to resolve the problem, I made a suggestion for change that my manager decided to implement.

- We got together as a team to try and find a better way of working that would benefit the organisation.

- I have worked in previous roles where there is a requirement to continually seek more efficient ways of doing things. On that basis, I understand the police service is an organisation that must continually look to develop and improve, and I would be someone who will embrace this important attribute innovatively and positively.

Takes an innovative and creative approach to solving problems.

- Whilst my work colleague's method of working had been satisfactory, I knew there was a better, more innovative way of solving the problem.

- The suggestions for improvement were innovative, and everyone within the team embraced the changes with a positive attitude.

- The method of working I decided to utilise was innovative.

- This new and innovative way of working proved to be of benefit to the company.

- I am someone who has a strong ability to solve problems by utilising creative thinking. For example, in my previous role, I frequently solved difficult problems by thinking outside of the box and by carefully analysing the information that was available.

26 Police Officer Core Competency Keywords, Phrases and Sentences

ROLE PLAYS

Positive about change, adapting rapidly to different ways of working and putting effort into making them work.

- In order to resolve the problem, I will need to try a different approach to the situation.
- To find the missing person, we will need to act quickly.
- I will take immediate action and ask people to stop what they are doing and search for the missing person.
- I can assure you we will do all we can to make this work. I will not stop until the situation is resolved satisfactorily.

Flexible and open to alternative approaches to solving problems.

- To solve this problem, I feel we need to try a different approach to working. Here is my proposal.
- I will maintain a flexible approach to solving this problem.
- I can assure you, sir, that if this method does not work, I will try a new and fresh approach until we achieve the desired outcome.
- This problem needs to be solved quickly and I have a number of plans to implement and try.
- I feel if we utilise a flexible approach to this problem, we will be able to solve it satisfactorily.

Finds better, more cost-effective ways to do things, making suggestions for change.

- I will now change my plan in order to solve the issue quickly.
- I will deploy resources in a specific area in order to improve the speed in which the situation is resolved.
- Once the situation is resolved, I will make suggestions to my supervisor so that improvements can be made for next time.

Takes an innovative and creative approach to solving problems.

- This problem is going to require an innovative approach in order to reach a successful conclusion.

- By using all of the information that is available to me, I have an innovative plan that will help solve the problem.

- The creative approach I will use to solve this problem is XYZ.

Competency #3
Service Delivery

SERVICE DELIVERY

The SERVICE DELIVERY competency is all about how you deliver effective service to the public. This requires an ability to plan, organise and take an objective approach to problem solving. As a serving police officer, you must be able to multi-task, cope well under pressure and focus intently on the desired outcome.

Here's what you'll be required to demonstrate not only during the selection process, but also once you become a police officer:

> Understands the organisation's objectives and priorities, and how own work fits into these. Plans and organises tasks effectively, taking a structured and methodical approach to achieving outcomes. Manages multiple tasks effectively by thinking things through in advance, prioritising and managing time well. Focuses on the outcomes to be achieved, working quickly and accurately and seeking guidance when appropriate.

Let's now take a look at my suggested keywords, phrases and sentences for the core competency of SERVICE DELIVERY.

APPLICATION FORM AND INTERVIEWS

Understands the organisation's objectives and priorities, and how own work fits into these.

- I decided to focus my actions on the objectives of my employer to achieve the best outcome.
- After reading the documentation carefully, I could then create a plan based on the individual's needs.
- After assessing the situation and making good use of the information I had available, I was then able to create an action plan based on the required objectives.
- I decided to prioritise each task based on the objectives of my employer.
- I understand how important it is as a police officer to work towards achieving the services objectives and to conduct my duties with professionalism, dedication and commitment.
- The police service works hard towards achieving important goals and objectives and I believe I can be relied upon to help the organisation deliver these efficiently to the public.

Plans and organises tasks effectively, taking a structured and methodical approach to achieving outcomes.

- I decided to create an action plan that would allow me to follow a structured approach to working. This would ensure that what I was doing would meet the needs of the individual.
- In order to meet the desired outcome, I knew I would need to create a focused plan of action.
- During each stage of the task I revisited the brief to make sure we were all following the agreed, structured plan.
- I implemented a methodical way of working which would ensure each task was completed on time and to the required standard.
- I have lots of experience working efficiently and effectively whilst carrying out important and pressurised tasks.
- I always strive to conduct my work professionally and competently whilst working towards my employer's goals and objectives.

Manages multiple tasks effectively by thinking things through in advance, prioritising and managing time well.

- Before I set to work on the task, I considered all options carefully and thought through the potential implications of my actions.

- As part of the plan, I knew we would need to work on, and complete, multiple tasks all at once. To achieve our goal, I allocated tasks based on each team member's strengths.

- Due to the fact we would need to manage multiple tasks all at once, I created a list to make sure each task was carried out in order of priority.

- During the project, I managed multiple tasks concurrently and made sure each one was completed to a high standard in line with the brief.

Focuses on the outcomes to be achieved, working quickly and accurately and seeking guidance when appropriate.

- I focused intently on the end goal and worked as fast as I could to make sure I achieved my aim.

- During the task, I wanted to seek clarification from my line manager to make sure what I was doing was accurate.

- Throughout each task, I made sure I checked my work carefully for professionalism and accuracy.

- I worked quickly and accurately at all times, and whenever I was unsure of a task, I would seek guidance from my line manager.

- As a police officer I promise to focus hard on achieving the organisation's objectives and outcomes, and would work at all times with great pride, professionalism, accuracy and speed.`

Competency #3 Service Delivery

ROLE PLAYS

Understands the organisation's objectives and priorities, and how own work fits into these.

- I have read the information available to me in detail and will focus my plan of action to make sure I follow all guidelines.
- The centre's guidelines state XYZ. On that basis, my proposed plan of action will be XYZ.
- The centre I work for has specific rules and procedures which I must follow at all times.
- It is important I follow the guidance notes and rules when dealing with this situation.

Plans and organises tasks effectively, taking a structured and methodical approach to achieving outcomes.

- In order to achieve the desired outcome, I am going to take a structured approach to working, which involves XYZ.
- I feel the best way to reach a successful resolution to this situation will be to prioritise what needs to be done and by whom.
- The most effective way to deal with this situation will be to take a structured approach to the task.

Manages multiple tasks effectively by thinking things through in advance, prioritising and managing time well.

- I will need to manage multiple tasks during this incident and, based on the needs of the situation, here is what we will do.
- To achieve my goal, I will allocate tasks to people within the centre who are best placed to deal with them effectively.
- Having carefully considered the information you have given me, I feel the best way forward based on priority is, XYZ.
- Having listened to you carefully, and considered the potential outcomes, here is what I plan to do.

Police Officer Core Competency Keywords, Phrases and Sentences

Focuses on the outcomes to be achieved, working quickly and accurately and seeking guidance when appropriate.

- I will contact the CCTV centre immediately and ask them to review any video footage they have available, which will in turn help me to make the right decision.

- It is important that we focus on the main goal here. Let's concentrate on the information available to us so we can reach the desired outcome.

- We will need to work very quickly and accurately if we are to find the missing child. On that basis, I will ask all security staff to monitor the exits.

- I will seek guidance from the police as to how they can assist us in dealing with this urgent situation.

Competency #4
Professionalism

PROFESSIONALISM

It goes without saying that police officers must act with integrity and professionalism at all times, whilst working towards the values and ethics laid down by the police service. I believe that, before you go through the selection process for becoming a police officer, you should study, learn and understand the values of your chosen force and be willing to abide by them. Every negative police-related story that features in the press and media undoes some of the great work done by the vast majority of police staff. Therefore, the police service only wants to employ police officers who will act with integrity, professionalism and strong ethics at all times whilst undertaking their duties. In addition to upholding the professional standards of the police service, you will also be required to act calmly at all times. As I am sure you are already aware, you will at times be placed under great pressure as a police officer, and the members of the public you serve will expect you to remain calm, professional and objective at all times. You will often be required to make difficult decisions whilst under extreme pressure, and you have to be confident you have the attributes and skills to do this.

Here's what you'll be required to demonstrate not only during the selection process, but also once you become a police officer:

> Acts with integrity, in line with the values and ethical standards of the Police Service. Takes ownership for resolving problems, demonstrating courage and resilience in dealing with difficult and potentially volatile situations. Acts on own initiative to address issues, showing a strong work ethic and demonstrating extra effort when required. Upholds professional standards, acting honestly and ethically, and challenges unprofessional conduct or discriminatory behaviour. Asks for and acts on feedback, learning from experience and developing own professional skills and knowledge. Remains calm and professional under pressure, defusing conflict and being prepared to step forward and take control when required.

Let's now take a look at my suggested keywords, phrases and sentences for the core competency of PROFESSIONALISM.

Competency #4 Professionalism

APPLICATION FORM AND INTERVIEWS

Acts with integrity, in line with the values and ethical standards of the Police Service. Takes ownership for resolving problems, demonstrating courage and resilience in dealing with difficult and potentially volatile situations.

- I decided it was important for me to take ownership of the situation with a view to resolving it as quickly and professionally as possible.

- Due to the fact that the situation could potentially deteriorate, I felt it necessary to intervene both safely and calmly.

- I acted professionally and ethically at all times during the situation.

- By acting with integrity at all times, I was able to see the situation through to a successful resolution.

- I fully understand the responsibility that comes with such a role and believe strongly I can be relied upon to uphold the principles, values and ethics of this police service.

- I have an ability to remain calm whilst under pressure and can be relied upon to follow my training and operational procedures during times of immense stress and pressure.

- As a police officer, I would carry out my duties professionally, diligently and in line with the values and ethics laid out by my employer.

- I understand the importance of remaining calm whilst under pressure and have plenty of experience in situations like this. I feel confident I will be able to uphold the principles, values and ethics of my chosen police constabulary and would ensure I consistently acted as a positive role model for the organisation I am serving.

38 Police Officer Core Competency Keywords, Phrases and Sentences

Acts on own initiative to address issues, showing a strong work ethic and demonstrating extra effort when required. Upholds professional standards, acting honestly and ethically, and challenges unprofessional conduct or discriminatory behaviour.

- I decided to take the initiative by volunteering to solve the problem. Throughout the entire experience, I worked hard and put in the extra hours to make sure everything was completed successfully.

- I immediately challenged his comments in a calm and confident manner. His comments were totally unacceptable, and it was important that I intervened to protect the individual.

- I acted with professionalism at all times and made sure the situation was safe and that nobody was in danger.

- By acting honestly and with integrity I was able to persuade both members of the team to see each other's point of view.

- I understand that the police service sets high standards and expects its police officers to demonstrate these at all times. I believe I can be relied upon to act as a positive role model for the organisation and would always act honestly and ethically whilst taking pride in my work.

Asks for and acts on feedback, learning from experience and developing own professional skills and knowledge.

- At the end of the project, I asked my manager for feedback, because I was keen to improve for next time.

- At the end of the situation, I analysed my performance and sought a number of ways I could improve for next time.

- Following previous feedback from my line manager, I decided to change the way I approached the situation.

- I decided to undertake a professional development course, so I could improve my skills, knowledge and expertise in this area.

- I am someone who continually looks to improve and develop and have consistently sought feedback from my previous employers. I see development as a key part of the role of a police officer and would embrace continuous development positively and enthusiastically.

Competency #4 Professionalism 39

Remains calm and professional under pressure, defusing conflict and being prepared to step forward and take control when required.

- Although the situation was pressurised, I knew it was important to remain calm at all times.

- I could detect the situation had the potential to escalate further, so I decided to take control with a view to defusing the conflict quickly and safely.

- As soon as I felt the situation starting to deteriorate, I stepped in and took control. This enabled me to offer suggestions for quickly resolving the conflict.

- I was aware that the situation had the potential to deteriorate, so I took control and steered the conversation away from the potential conflict.

- I am someone who can be relied upon to work calmly under pressure and would always carry out my duties professionally and responsibly. I am also someone who will step up and take control of situations when required and would always follow my training, abiding by operational procedures and standards at all times.

ROLE PLAYS

Acts with integrity, in line with the values and ethical standards of the Police Service. Takes ownership for resolving problems, demonstrating courage and resilience in dealing with difficult and potentially volatile situations.

- I will take responsibility for the situation, and on that basis, here is what I propose.

- I can totally understand your frustrations (sir/madam). However, in order to resolve this situation quickly and safely, I will stick to my original plan of action which I feel is best for all parties concerned.

- It is very important that I follow the guidelines, standards and operating procedures defined by the centre.

- It is important that we all remain calm. I will take ownership of this situation so that it reaches a successful conclusion.

- It is important that I act with professionalism at all times, and in order to do that, I will follow the rules, guidelines and code of ethics laid out by the centre.

Acts on own initiative to address issues, showing a strong work ethic and demonstrating extra effort when required. Upholds professional standards, acting honestly and ethically, and challenges unprofessional conduct or discriminatory behaviour.

- Please do not use that type of language, sir. If you continue, I am afraid I will be required to call the police. It is my intention to help you, but I must ask you to refrain from using aggressive language. Thank you.

- I can understand how you feel, sir. However, if we are to reach a satisfactory solution that you are happy with, I must ask you to remain calm and stop using inappropriate language. It is important that we all adhere to the Equality Policy guidelines as laid out by the centre.

- I believe the best course of action is to follow the guidelines and advice contained within my organisation's code of conduct.

Asks for and acts on feedback, learning from experience and developing own professional skills and knowledge.

- Can I ask you, madam? Does my proposed solution work for you in this particular situation?

- I thank you for your feedback and I will certainly take on-board your comments, which I pass on to my senior manager as soon as possible.

- I believe the person has acted inappropriately, and on that basis, I will arrange for training to be conducted so they can learn from this experience.

Remains calm and professional under pressure, defusing conflict and being prepared to step forward and take control when required.

- If I could just ask you to slow down sir and explain in a calm manner exactly what has happened?

- I will now ask you a series of questions that will enable me to solve the problem quickly and to your satisfaction.

- Your comments are not in line with the centre's Equality Policy, and on that basis, I must ask you to stop.

- Before this situation escalates further, let's take a moment to focus on the key facts so we can find an appropriate resolution.

Competency #5
Decision Making

DECISION MAKING

As a police officer you will be required to make difficult decisions, often whilst under pressure. When you are called to potentially life-threatening incidents, you will need to take control of the situation and gather the information and facts available to you before making very important decisions. As the incident develops, and the situation changes, you will need to balance the risks and change your plan of action accordingly.

Here's what you'll be required to demonstrate not only during the selection process, but also once you become a police officer:

> Gathers, verifies and assesses all appropriate and available information to gain an accurate understanding of situations. Considers a range of possible options before making clear, timely, justifiable decisions. Reviews decisions in the light of new information and changing circumstances. Balances risks, costs and benefits, thinking about the wider impact of decisions. Exercises discretion and applies professional judgement, ensuring actions and decisions are proportionate and in the public interest.

Let's now take a look at my suggested keywords, phrases and sentences for the core competency of DECISION MAKING.

Competency #5 Decision Making

APPLICATION FORM AND INTERVIEWS

Gathers, verifies and assesses all appropriate and available information to gain an accurate understanding of situations. Considers a range of possible options before making clear, timely, justifiable decisions.

- I decided to gather as much information as possible, as this would enable me to make the right decision for the team moving forward.

- Before making my decision, I considered a range of options.

- I felt the decision I made was justifiable given the nature of the problem and the information I was presented with.

- In order to make an accurate decision that would benefit everyone, I decided to gather, assess and disseminate as much information as possible.

- I understand that, as a police officer, I will be responsible for my actions and I can be relied upon to make justifiable decisions based on factual information and a clear assessment of the situation I am in.

- I believe I am a strong decision maker who will not make unjustified or rash decisions, especially whilst under pressure. I know it is very important to make the right decisions based on the information and facts available.

Reviews decisions in the light of new information and changing circumstances. Balances risks, costs and benefits, thinking about the wider impact of decisions.

- Part way through the project we encountered a problem, and so I decided to review the initial plan so appropriate changes could be made in order to meet the pre-determined goal.

- Once the new information had been gathered, I decided to review it carefully to ensure the initial plan was the correct one.

- During the rapidly changing situation I was in, I continually reassessed the information I was receiving and adapted my plan of action accordingly.

- Using the information I had available to me, I was able to make a balanced decision that would see a risk-free outcome for all involved.

- At every stage of the process, I considered the wider implications for my decisions.

- As a police officer you have the responsibility to think carefully about the outcome of your actions and decisions, and how they can impact on the wider organisation as a whole.

Exercises discretion and applies professional judgement, ensuring actions and decisions are proportionate and in the public interest.

- Once I had obtained all of the relevant information needed, I created a plan of action that was in the interests of everyone involved.

- The information I had received was confidential, and on that basis, it was important for me not to share that with the other members of the team.

- Using my professional judgement, I felt the best decision that could be made was XYZ.

- The action I was taking was proportionate to the situation that I found myself in.

- I fully understand that police officers are required to ensure the decisions they make are in the public interest and I will always act as a positive, trustworthy and reliable member of the service if I am successful.

ROLE PLAYS

Gathers, verifies and assesses all appropriate and available information to gain an accurate understanding of situations. Considers a range of possible options before making clear, timely, justifiable decisions.

- I have now gathered all of the information available, and on that basis, I will use it to create a plan of action moving forward.
- In order for me to gather, verify and assess the situation, I will need to ask you a number of questions.
- Based on the information you have given me, we will need to act very quickly in order to resolve the situation safely.
- Now that you have given me all of the information needed, I just want to confirm a couple of points to make sure what you are telling me is accurate and correct.

Reviews decisions in the light of new information and changing circumstances. Balances risks, costs and benefits, thinking about the wider impact of decisions.

- The information you have just provided me with is now different to what was initially discussed. On that basis, I will suggest a different course of action.
- The situation has now developed further and in response to this, I will take the following course of action.
- Having had the time to gather and review the information you have given to me, I suggest the following course of action.
- The decision I make will need to take into consideration the wider implications for you personally. On that basis, I suggest XYZ.

Exercises discretion and applies professional judgement, ensuring actions and decisions are proportionate and in the public interest.

- I can assure you that the information you have provided me with will stay confidential.

- Based on the information provided, I feel the most appropriate course of action we should take is XYZ. This, I feel, is in the best interests of all involved.

- Using my professional judgement, I feel the best course of action is XYZ.

- The course of action I am about to take is proportionate to the situation.

Competency #6
Working With Others

WORKING WITH OTHERS

Being part of the wider police service team and working together towards the organisation's goals is a very important aspect of the police officer's role. Working with others is essentially 'teamwork'; however, it also incorporates the requirement to work with people not just within your team, but also from other external organisations who may have a vested interest in the police, such as the fire service, local authority, or social services.

Here's what you'll be required to demonstrate not only during the selection process, but also once you become a police officer:

> Works co-operatively with others to get things done, willingly giving help and support to colleagues. Is approachable, developing positive working relationships. Explains things well, focusing on the key points and talking to people using language they understand. Listens carefully and asks questions to clarify understanding, expressing own views positively and constructively. Persuades people by stressing the benefits of a particular approach, keeps them informed of progress and manages their expectations. Is courteous, polite and considerate, showing empathy and compassion. Deals with people as individuals and addresses their specific needs and concerns. Treats people with respect and dignity, dealing with them fairly and without prejudice regardless of their background or circumstances.

Let's now take a look at my suggested keywords, phrases and sentences for the core competency of WORKING WITH OTHERS.

APPLICATION FORM AND INTERVIEWS

Works co-operatively with others to get things done, willingly giving help and support to colleagues. Is approachable, developing positive working relationships.

- During the task I decided to work closely with the other members of the team.

- Throughout the team task, I supported my colleagues as I knew this would enable us to complete the job quickly and professionally.

- I maintained strong lines of communication between myself and my work colleagues, as this ensured those who needed support would get it quickly.

- My team mate asked for help and I immediately went over to support her.

- During the team task it became apparent that one member of our group was struggling. I immediately stopped what I was doing and went over to assist them.

- I am a competent and experienced team worker who enjoys working with others to achieve the goals and priorities of my employer.

- I have plenty of experience working as part of a wider team and believe I possess the right skills, qualities and attributes to work in collaboration with others, to achieve time-sensitive tasks.

Explains things well, focusing on the key points and talking to people using language they understand. Listens carefully and asks questions to clarify understanding, expressing own views positively and constructively.

- During the initial team brief, I explained things in a coherent and simple manner.

- Once the initial team brief was complete, I asked everyone if they understood what was required.

- I started to ask the lady a number of questions to make sure I fully understood the situation and her concerns.

- Although the person disagreed with me, I put across my argument positively and constructively.

- At all times I listened to the customer carefully, and utilised probing questions to get to the bottom of their complaint.

- I am a confident communicator who listens carefully to the task in hand, and will always contribute positively when the need arises.

Competency #6 Working With Others

Persuades people by stressing the benefits of a particular approach, keeps them informed of progress and manages their expectations. Is courteous, polite and considerate, showing empathy and compassion.

- Whilst talking to the individual, I tried to explain the benefits of my approach.

- Once I had gathered all of the necessary information, I contacted the customer again to update them on the progress I had made.

- I could detect the gentleman was feeling upset, and so I utilised empathy and showed compassion at all times.

- It was clear the customer's expectations were high, and on that basis, I made no false promises and I kept in constant communication with her at all times.

- The customer I was dealing with had very high expectations, and so I explained the potential outcomes to her in a clear and concise manner to ensure she was fully aware of all the possible resolutions to the situation.

- I understand that, as a police officer, I will be required to demonstrate empathy and compassion at times and will always work hard to serve the public professionally, competently and with enthusiasm.

Deals with people as individuals and addresses their specific needs and concerns. Treats people with respect and dignity, dealing with them fairly and without prejudice regardless of their background or circumstances.

- At all times I treated the person with respect.

- I could understand how the person must have been feeling, and on that basis, I modified my approach to dealing with their complaint.

- After I had gathered all of the available information, I started to address the gentleman's concerns, focusing purely on his needs at that particular time.

- Regardless of their circumstances, I treated them fairly and with respect at all times.

- The lady felt that the previous person she spoke to had treated her unfairly. Throughout my conversations with her, I treated her respectfully and fairly at all times and kept her updated on progress as it happened.

- As a police officer, I understand I will be required to treat people with dignity and respect at all times and I can be relied upon to uphold the values and standards laid out by the police service.

ROLE PLAYS

Works co-operatively with others to get things done, willingly giving help and support to colleagues. Is approachable, developing positive working relationships.

- In order to resolve this situation, I will need to work closely with the other members of the centre.

- There are a number of members within our wider team, and on that basis, I will work with them closely to find the missing person.

- At all times you can contact me at the Customer Services Centre. I will make myself available whenever you need me and I will keep you updated on progress as and when it happens.

- It is my job to support you during this difficult time and I will be here to answer any questions you may have.

Explains things well, focusing on the key points and talking to people using language they understand. Listens carefully and asks questions to clarify understanding, expressing own views positively and constructively.

- I will now explain to you exactly what is going to happen.

- Please explain to me what you saw. As you are speaking, I will listen carefully and take notes.

- I want to clarify a few things you have told me, just to make sure I am getting the correct information.

- Do you understand my proposed plan of action? Is everything clear?

- Before moving on and implementing my proposed plan of action, I want to ensure you fully understand the possible outcomes of the situation.

Persuades people by stressing the benefits of a particular approach, keeps them informed of progress and manages their expectations. Is courteous, polite and considerate, showing empathy and compassion.

- Let me explain the benefits of my approach to working.

- I will keep you informed of my progress at all times and you can also contact me here at the Customer Service Centre whenever you need me.

- Whilst I can understand your frustrations, the centre's policy is there to protect everyone, both employees and customers.

- The result of my actions will be XYZ.

Deals with people as individuals and addresses their specific needs and concerns. Treats people with respect and dignity, dealing with them fairly and without prejudice regardless of their background or circumstances.

- Is there anything within my proposed plan of action you feel uncomfortable with?

- Are you satisfied with my proposed plan of action?

- I want to make sure I treat you with dignity and respect. Is there anything I have said that causes you concern?

- I would like to gather as much information as possible, as this will help me to solve the issues and also address your concerns.

- If at any point during our conversation, anything is unclear, or if you have any questions, please feel free to ask and I will do all I can to assist you.

- In order to build a positive relationship with all store owners and visitors who come to the centre, we have an Equality Policy that covers what type of behaviour is unacceptable and the steps a person can take if they wish to make a complaint.

- If there is anything I have said that comes across as confusing or ambiguous, please let me know and I will provide further clarification.

Sample Application Form Question & Answer (Competencies 1-6)

58 Police Officer Core Competency Keywords, Phrases and Sentences

SAMPLE POLICE OFFICER APPLICATION FORM QUESTION & ANSWER

In this next short section of your guide, I am going to provide you with a sample police officer application form question and answer. The answer provided is how I personally would respond to the question and is my attempt at matching the core competencies that are relevant to the role of a police officer. I have not utilised any of the keywords, phrases or sentences covered in the guide. Instead, I have created my own unique answer that I believe is a close match to the assessable competencies.

It is important that you create your own answers to the questions contained in your police officer application form, but I hope the following answer will give you an idea of the standard to aim for. You will notice the question below requires you to explain what **knowledge**, **skills** and **experience** you have that will enable you to meet the requirements of a police officer. In order to answer the question correctly, I have covered all three of these areas within my response. Please do not use this exact response on your own application form.

What knowledge, skills and experiences do you have that will enable you to meet the requirements of a police officer?

> I have studied in detail the police officer core competencies in order to gain a thorough understanding of what the role involves and how I will be required to perform if I become a police officer. Having studied the competencies, I believe I have all of the attributes required to serve the public and act as a positive role model for the police service. In addition to the core competencies, I have studied and researched the police service values in respect of how I will be required to perform and operate on a daily basis. I believe I can make a positive contribution to the organisation and work hard, with others, to meet the needs of the community in which I am serving.
>
> My skills are numerous and varied. For example, I am able to deliver quality service whilst focusing on the needs of individuals and also working towards my employer's goals. If a team is not working well, I have the skillset to break down barriers and encourage people to work together to achieve the main aims of the organisation. I enjoy working in a rapidly changing environment and I embrace change and all that it brings with it. I am able to remain calm, composed and confident in all

Sample Application Form Question & Answer (Competencies 1-6)

situations and have the ability to make informed decisions utilising the information at my disposal. My skills also include an ability to plan and organise my work effectively whilst also changing my approach to tasks if the need arises. I am able to act with integrity at all times and understand how my actions impact on the reputation of the organisation I am working for.

My experience includes working with other people as part of a team to achieve difficult tasks. Being able to work both unsupervised, and also as part of a wider team supporting those who need help in the process. I have many years' experience making difficult and pressurised decisions based on numerous sources of information. For example, in my previous role as a customer service officer, I was required on a daily basis to gather and assess multiple streams of information and utilise these to make important customer-focused decisions. I have lots of experience working in a diverse organisation and I treat people fairly and consistently at all times. I am a competent communicator and never make rash or ill-informed decisions. I understand the responsibilities that come with being a police officer and I strongly believe my skills, knowledge and experience will be an asset to your trusted organisation.

SAMPLE ASSESSMENT CENTRE INTERVIEW QUESTION AND ANSWER

In this next short section of your guide, I will provide you with a sample police officer assessment centre interview question and answer, once again, to show you how I personally would prepare my answers in line with the assessable core competencies. When preparing for the police officer assessment centre interview questions, I recommend you utilise the STAR technique for structuring your answers. Here is a breakdown of the STAR technique and how each element is used to provide solid, genuine answers:

SITUATION

Tell the interview panel what the specific situation was that you were in.

TASK

Now tell the interview panel what had to be done.

ACTION

Now move on and tell the interview panel what action you decided to take, and also what action other people took.

RESULT

Tell the interview panel what the result or outcome was following yours and other's actions. The result should always be positive.

NOTE: It is also good practice to explain at the end how you reflected upon your performance to look for ways you could improve or develop for next time. This is usually called the 'REFLECTIVE' stage.

I have now provided you with a sample assessment centre interview question and answer that utilises the STAR technique with the added 'reflection' element at the end. Please do not use this exact response during your own interview.

Sample Application Form Question & Answer (Competencies 1-6)

DESCRIBE A TIME WHEN YOU CHALLENGED SOMEONE'S BEHAVIOR THAT WAS EITHER INAPPROPRIATE OR DISCRIMINATORY?

Whilst at work one afternoon, I was taking a break in the canteen when I overheard one of my experienced work colleagues being rude and offensive to a female member of staff. In line with my organisation's values and code of conduct, this type of behaviour is not acceptable and so I decided to step in and take action.

It was my duty to take ownership of the situation, ask my work colleague to stop his behaviour and also explain to him why it was unacceptable. In order to achieve this, I would need to be resilient and remain calm and composed at all times.

I walked over calmly to the table and sat down with my co-worker. I explained to him that I found his comments offensive and that I would like him to stop. He immediately took offence to my comments and told me to mind my own business. I remained calm, composed and started to explain how his actions were against our organisation's values and code of ethics. I also explained that the lady would most probably find his comments inappropriate, too.

As soon as I referred to the organisation's code of ethics and values, his attitude changed, and he apologised for his behaviour. I then went on to explain to him why his comments were not acceptable in the modern world where we are all required to treat each other with respect and dignity. He thanked me for my input and promised me he would learn from the situation.

Upon reflection, I felt I handled the situation well. However, it may have been appropriate to speak to my work colleague in private, away from everyone else in the canteen, once I had asked him to stop. I always reflect upon my performance and will always look for ways to improve and develop.

New Police Officer Core Competencies

NEW POLICE OFFICER CORE COMPETENCIES

There are a number of police services who are now utilising different core competencies than the ones I covered within the initial sections of this guide. These include the Metropolitan Police Service and others.

To ensure I cover all of the possible core competencies utilised up and down the country, I will now provide you will sample keywords, phrases and sentences based on these new competencies. For obvious reasons, please only use these if they are applicable to the application and assessment process for your chosen police service. The competencies I will be covering over the next few sections are as follows:

- Emotionally aware
- Taking ownership
- Working collaboratively
- Deliver, support and inspire
- Analyse critically
- Innovative and open minded

Competency #7
Emotionally Aware

COMPETENCY #7 – EMOTIONALLY AWARE

As a police officer you will need to be emotionally aware. This is in respect of your own emotions, and the emotions of others. You will often be required to work under extreme and pressurised situations, and to do so will take courage, determination and an ability to control your emotions. You will be expected to remain calm and exhibit strong decision-making skills. You will also be expected to treat people, particularly members of the public, with respect and compassion and acknowledge people's differing views, beliefs and opinions. You should also be aware of your own limitations and ask for help when you feel necessary. At no point should you make decisions that could endanger the lives of your colleagues or the public you are serving.

Here's what you'll be required to demonstrate not only during the selection process, but also once you become a police officer:

> It's very important for police officers to be emotionally aware. Not only do you need to be emotionally aware towards the needs and feelings of others, but you also need to be emotionally aware of yourself. You must be able to control your emotions when under high amounts of pressure, and exhibit strong levels of decision making. Police work is highly stressful, and will push you to your limits. Therefore, it's vital that police employees can stay calm and collected, and manage their emotions.
>
> - Treating others with respect and compassion.
>
> - Acknowledging other people's opinions, values and beliefs – provided they fall within lawful boundaries.
>
> - Asking for help when necessary.
>
> - Recognising your own limitations, and seeking assistance in accordance with this.

Let's now take a look at my suggested keywords, phrases and sentences for the core competency of EMOTIONALLY AWARE. You will notice I have simply provided you with a list for the application form/interviews and a list for the role play scenarios. I believe each of these sentences will help you demonstrate the core competency of being emotionally aware through what you write and say during the selection process.

Competency #7 Emotionally Aware

APPLICATION FORM AND INTERVIEWS

- At all times, I was aware how my actions could impact the situation. On that basis, I chose my words carefully to ensure I maintained control of the problem.

- I wanted to ensure the lady felt respected at all times. To achieve this, I asked her probing questions about how she was feeling, which in turn, allowed me to demonstrate compassion and respect.

- After listening to the gentleman carefully, I felt his views and opinions were valid. I acknowledged how he must have been feeling before deciding on the appropriate course of action.

- Throughout dealing with the situation, I continually acknowledged the customers' views and beliefs and respected their concerns whenever they were raised.

- I could detect the person was very upset about what had just happened to them, and so I spent some time providing emotional support as and when it was needed. Moving forward, the decisions I made focused on ensuring their beliefs and opinions were catered for.

- During the project I was unsure on how to complete a particular complex task. To make sure I didn't do anything wrong, I sought advice from my line manager.

- Whilst carrying out the team task, I was concerned I was not sufficiently qualified for one particular element. So that I didn't put the team or project in jeopardy, I asked a suitably qualified work colleague to assist me.

- I am aware that police officers are required to make challenging and difficult decisions on a regular basis, and I can be relied upon to be an effective decision-maker, taking into consideration people's views and opinions in the process.

- I am a strong decision maker, but I also have the ability to understand my own limitations and would always seek clarification or advice when needed. At no point would I put my colleagues or the public in danger and would always follow my training and operational procedures.

- Although I am a strong and confident decision maker, I also have the ability to demonstrate compassion, understanding and empathy when the situation arises. I am completely respectful of others, and would also acknowledge and take into consideration people's differing views, opinions and beliefs.

ROLE PLAYS

- "I need to consider how my actions will impact the situation. To help me make the right decision, I would like to ask you some probing questions."

- "I can tell you are very upset. Please tell me how you feel and how the other person's actions have impacted your beliefs and values?"

- "Is there anything within my proposed plan of action that has a negative impact on your views or beliefs?"

- "In order to help me achieve the end goal, I will need to ask a member of my team for assistance."

- "I am not in a position to make that decision. However, I will ask my senior manager if the change you have recommended can be made."

- "I can see this situation has impacted you from an emotional perspective and I am concerned for your welfare. I can assure you my decisions moving forward will take into consideration your views and opinions and I will be respectful of your beliefs."

- "I am concerned for your welfare and will ask for assistance from the medical centre who are situated right here at the centre. In the meantime, please take a seat and tell me exactly what has happened."

- "I can totally understand how the person's comments have had an impact on you from an emotional perspective, and I fully sympathise with how you must be feeling. I can assure you I will deal with this situation robustly and in line with the centre's policy on harassment."

Competency #8
Taking Ownership

COMPETENCY #8 – TAKING OWNERSHIP

As you can imagine, police officers are required to take ownership of situations and incidents they attend. In addition to this, they are also required to take ownership of their emotions, any mistakes they make and also look for ways to continually improve, learn and develop. Honesty and integrity are also very important aspects of the police officer role and the competency of TAKING OWNERSHIP will assess all of these qualities and traits.

Here's what you'll be required to demonstrate not only during the selection process, but also once you become a police officer:

> In order to work as a police officer, it's vital that you can take ownership and responsibility, and hold yourself accountable for your own actions. Part of this means accepting that sometimes minor mistakes will happen, but the way you deal with these is what is important. You must learn from your mistakes, and seek improvement-based feedback. Furthermore, it's critical that you can take pride in your work, and recognise your own limitations.
>
> - Accurately identifying and then responding to problems/issues.
>
> - Completing tasks with enthusiasm and positivity.
>
> - Taking responsibility for their own decisions.
>
> - Providing others with helpful and constructive feedback on their working practice.

Let's now take a look at my suggested keywords, phrases and sentences for the core competency of TAKING OWNERSHIP. You will notice I have simply provided you with a list for the application form/interviews and a list for the role play scenarios. I believe each of these sentences will help you demonstrate the core competency of TAKING OWNERSHIP through what you write and say during the selection process.

Competency #8 Taking Ownership

APPLICATION FORM AND INTERVIEWS

- I decided to take ownership and control of the situation, as I knew I could achieve a successful outcome.

- The only way the task could be completed on time and to the required standard, was to work hard as a team and be positive about the outcome. I knew that if we all worked with enthusiasm and commitment, we could complete the task on time.

- The initial decision I had made was not working, so I decided to go back to the drawing board and create a new plan that took into consideration what I had learned so far.

- Part way through the team task, I could tell things were not working, so I decided to change the plan with a new set of working practices. This would ensure the end goal was completed successfully.

- My work colleague was not contributing effectively to the team task, so I spoke to him in private to see if anything was wrong and to also encourage him to help the rest of the team meet our targets.

- I can be relied upon to take full responsibility and ownership, not just for my actions, but also my own development and progress as a police officer for the service I will be representing.

- I am an honest person who can be relied upon to act with integrity and professionalism at all times. I enjoy taking responsibility and ownership of my own personal development. If I ever make a mistake, I will acknowledge it, put it right and then look to improve so the same mistake does not happen again.

- I always accept constructive feedback in a positive and enthusiastic manner, as I am aware that by doing so, I am not only improving my own skills and qualities, but I am also improving the level of service I provide for my employer.

ROLE PLAYS

- "I will now take ownership of this situation to make sure things get sorted out quickly and in line with the organisation's code of conduct."

- "OK, I will need to work with other members of the centre to find the missing person. If we work hard, and with focused determination and enthusiasm, then I am sure we can find them quickly."

- "Now that you have provided me with this new information, I will need to change my plan in order to reach the desired outcome."

- "I can totally understand your frustrations and I will speak to the specific member of the team to explain how his actions are not acceptable. Additional training will be provided where needed."

- "I take full responsibility for everything that happens from a customer service perspective and I will do all I can to investigate and resolve this complaint in line with my organisation's guidelines and rules."

- "I always take great pride in the fact our visitors can come to the centre and feel safe. On that basis, I will take immediate action to ensure this problem is resolved quickly. I will keep you fully updated on progress as and when I have some news."

- "How you have operated whilst here at the centre is against the rules and guidelines indicated in our policies. On that basis, I must ask you to stop doing this immediately. Moving forward, if you have any questions relating to how you should be operating whilst here at the centre as a store owner, please contact me here at the customer services desk and I will be more than happy to offer feedback and advice."

- "I believe on this occasion we have made a mistake and we will take your feedback onboard with a view to improving the way we do things at the centre moving forward."

Competency #9
Working Collaboratively

COMPETENCY #9 – WORKING COLLABORATIVELY

As a police officer you will have the responsibility of working closely with many different groups of people. Not just your work colleagues within the police service, but also with external individuals, teams and organisations who are all striving to deliver effective and efficient services to the public. Many years ago, some public sector organisations used to work in isolation, unaware of the potential that collaborative working can bring. More recently, it is a fundamental requirement of public sector services to work together to provide more cost effective, efficient and professional services that utilise combined resources and an intelligent sharing of information/data. For example, if social services hold important information about an individual that can assist the police either in the way they investigate crimes, or how they can support the community in which they serve, then it makes perfect sense for this information to be responsibly shared in line with GDPR best practice.

Here's what you'll be required to demonstrate not only during the selection process, but also once you become a police officer:

> Teamwork is a fundamental part of working as a police officer, and the better you can work as part of a collaborative unit, the better level of service you can provide to the public. Good police work is about building partnerships, not just with your colleagues, but with members of the public too. You must be polite and respectful with every person that you meet, and show that the police value the ideals of teamwork, collaboration and social unity.
>
> - Working cooperatively and in harmony with colleagues and professionals from other organisations.
>
> - Exhibiting an approachable and friendly exterior, so that others feel comfortable asking you for help or guidance.
>
> - Showing a genuine interest and appreciation in other people, their views and opinions, in order to build comradery and rapport.
>
> - Treating every person that you meet as an individual.

Let's now take a look at my suggested keywords, phrases and sentences for the core competency of WORKING COLLABORATIVELY. You will notice I have simply provided you with a list for the application form/interviews and a list for the role play scenarios. I believe each of these sentences will help you demonstrate the core competency of WORKING COLLABORATIVELY through what you write and say during the selection process.

APPLICATION FORM AND INTERVIEWS

- I worked closely with the other members of the team to make sure the task was completed on time and to specification. I knew that if I didn't work collaboratively with other key members, the task would not be completed correctly.

- At all times I maintained a friendly and open approach whilst dealing with the customer, as this would enable me to resolve their complaint quickly and in line with my organisation's code of ethics.

- I have a genuine interest in other people and will always strive to build positive relationships with those I meet through work or otherwise.

- I was genuinely concerned for the lady and wanted to make sure the situation was resolved to her satisfaction as quickly as possible.

- I was genuinely interested in how the customer was feeling, and so I asked probing questions to get to the bottom of the situation, as I wanted to prevent it from happening again.

- The new member of the team appeared unsettled due to being in unfamiliar surroundings. I went out of my way to introduce myself and to also make them feel welcomed and supported.

- I understand the importance of working together with both work colleagues and external stakeholders and can be relied upon to build positive relationships with everyone I am required to serve or to work alongside.

- Having previously worked closely as part of a team, with all members striving towards the same goal, I understand the importance of collaborative working, and that the mission of the police service I want to work for can only be achieved by building positive and long-lasting relationships.

ROLE PLAYS

- "I believe that, if I work closely with the other members of my team, I will then be able to resolve this situation quickly."

- "I can appreciate your frustrations and how you must be feeling, sir. However, please be assured that as the Customer Services Officer, I will do all I can to resolve this quickly for you."

- "I can only imagine how this incident must have made you feel. As the Customer Services Officer, I will make sure this situation is resolved quickly and that it does not happen again."

- "Having listened carefully to your concerns, I can now totally understand how that must have made you feel. I can assure you I will work closely with the other members of the centre to get this situation resolved as quickly as possible."

- "Once I have successfully gathered all of the information from you, I will then consider my plan of action and how I can resolve this problem by working in conjunction with other members of the centre."

- "If at any point during our conversation, anything is unclear, or if you have any questions, please feel free to ask and I will do all I can to assist you."

- "In order to build a positive relationship with all store owners and visitors who come to the centre, we have an Equality Policy that covers what type of behaviour is unacceptable and the steps a person can take if they wish to make a complaint."

- "If there is anything I have said that comes across as confusing or ambiguous, please let me know and I will provide further clarification."

Competency #10
Analyse Critically

COMPETENCY #10 ANALYSE CRITICALLY

As you can imagine, the only way a police officer can make effective decisions is to analyse the information they have available to them carefully and critically. You will need to gather the facts and information available during each scenario you deal with, before taking time-sensitive and evidence-based actions utilising your training, skills and expertise. If a police officer makes rash or foolish decisions, this can have dire consequences and it can also impact on the positive work the police service does in building its public reputation. Therefore, you will need to demonstrate during the selection process that you have the ability to use logic, reasoning, and only make decisions and take actions that you can justify later on.

Here's what you'll be required to demonstrate not only during the selection process, but also once you become a police officer:

> Working as a police officer involves large amounts of critical analysis. You'll be presented with a wide variety of data, and will need to use all of this data to come to informed decisions. This is essentially what 'taking an evidence-based approach' means. It's about using the evidence available to you effectively and efficiently, to gather as many facts and hard info as possible, before using this data in the most logical way.
>
> - Understanding the importance of critical thinking, analysis and careful consideration before making decisions.
>
> - Assessing and analysing information in an efficient and accurate manner.
>
> - Solving problems by using logic and sound reasoning.
>
> - Balancing out the advantages and disadvantages of actions, before taking them.
>
> - Recognising and pointing out flaws in data or information.

Let's now take a look at my suggested keywords, phrases and sentences for the core competency of ANALYSE CRITICALLY. You will notice I have simply provided you with a list for the application form/interviews and a list for the role play scenarios. I believe each of these sentences will help you demonstrate the core competency of ANALYSE CRITICALLY through what you write and say during the selection process.

Competency #10 Analyse Critically

APPLICATION FORM AND INTERVIEWS

- Before making my decision, I considered, utilised and assessed all of the information available to me.

- Before deciding on the appropriate course of action, I gathered all of the facts, details and information that was available. I knew this would be an important factor in the decision-making process.

- I felt it was important to use logic and clear thinking when making my decision. In order to achieve this, I gathered all of the necessary facts and information and then set about creating my plan of action.

- Once I had gathered all of the information available, and I had read the project brief in detail, I considered the advantages and disadvantages of each proposed course of action.

- Whilst reading the brief that had been provided by my manager, I noticed a potential problem that could impact on the outcome of the team task. I immediately raised this with my manager, so she could make an informed decision on the way forward.

- I understand how important it is as a police officer to be able to make decisions based on the facts I have available, and I will always follow my training and do all I can to uphold the principles of the service, continuing to build positive relationships with the community in which I am serving.

- I have the ability to carefully analyse and critically assess information that is put my way, and will always carry out my duties responsibly and in a manner that I can justify.

- In my previous role, I was consistently required to act only on the information I had available and would regularly exercise the process of balancing risk versus outcomes, with a view to operating justifiably and safely at all times.

ROLE PLAYS

- "Before I suggest a plan of action, I will need to gather as much information as possible. Please explain clearly exactly what has happened?"

- "Now that you have answered all of my questions and provided clarity on the situation, here is what I will do."

- "In order to locate the missing child, I want to apply logic and clear thinking to the situation. On that basis, I will contact the security team and ask them to cover every exit located at the centre to look out for the child."

- "Having assessed all of the information available to me, and considered the advantages and disadvantages of my plan, here is what I propose."

- "There are a number of advantages to be gained from working with other departments here within the centre. Having considered the facts, I will ask them to help me resolve this situation."

- "I have now had the time to analyse the facts I have available. I believe the most responsible and time-efficient method for dealing with this problem is XYZ."

- "The most logical way to deal with your complaint is to follow the standards and principles set out by the centre. On that basis, I will take the following action."

- "Based on the evidence you have given me, I feel the most logical and responsible steps to take are XYZ. This will enable us to resolve the problem in the fastest way possible, without putting anyone at harm or risk."

Competency #11
Deliver, Support & Inspire

COMPETENCY #11 - DELIVER, SUPPORT & INSPIRE

Deliver, support and inspire! Three fantastic words that, in my opinion, sum up the modern-day police officer. In a world where expectations of public services are at an all-time high, the ability to deliver exceptional service, whilst also supporting your teammates and inspiring the public to trust in you, is absolutely vital. It will be your job as a police officer to fully understand how your work and actions contribute to the wider vision of the police service. In order to achieve this, you must understand what the wider vision is, and I strongly recommend you study the values of the police service you are applying to join.

Here's what you'll be required to demonstrate not only during the selection process, but also once you become a police officer:

> It's imperative that police officers understand the wider vision of the police service. You must use the police's values in your day-to-day work, and show a dedication to working in the best interests of the public. Your positive contribution to the police is extremely important. Police officers must show an understanding of how their behaviour impacts on the reputation of the service, and strive to make a positive contribution to this at all times. You must be focused on helping your teammates to achieve high standards, whilst maintaining your own.
>
> - Being willing and ready to tackle challenging tasks, with the aim of improving the output of the police service.
>
> - Demonstrating an understanding of how their work contributes to the police as a whole.
>
> - Taking a conscientious and resilient approach to police work, always endeavouring to provide the best possible service.
>
> - Using resources efficiently, to make a significant impact.

Let's now take a look at my suggested keywords, phrases and sentences for the core competency of DELIVER, SUPPORT & INSPIRE. You will notice I have simply provided you with a list for the application form/interviews and a list for the role play scenarios. I believe each of these sentences will help you demonstrate the core competency of DELIVER, SUPPORT & INSPIRE through what you write and say during the selection process.

APPLICATION FORM AND INTERVIEWS

- At all times I was aware of how my actions could impact on my employer's reputation. Therefore, at all times, I communicated with professionalism and a friendly manner.

- I was fully aware at all times of my employer's values and code of conduct whilst dealing with the customer. I wanted to make sure my employer's reputation was not damaged by the mistake that had been made.

- Throughout the situation, I focused on providing outstanding customer service at all times and communicated with the customer in a positive and enthusiastic manner.

- Whilst dealing with the customer, I continually looked for ways to build trust and develop a positive working relationship by providing exceptional support and customer service at all times.

- Although the situation was challenging, I saw this as an opportunity to provide outstanding service by building trust with the customer and enhancing the reputation of my employer.

- I considered all resources at my disposal to make sure the task I was undertaking was cost effective and value for money for my organisation.

- I fully understood that if I did not complete the project successfully and on time for my employer, there could be negative connotations.

- I am someone who enjoys working in challenging and difficult circumstances and can be relied upon to act in a manner that is representative of the values the service sets. Through my actions, I will always uphold the principles, standards and ethics determined by my employer and will look to build positive relationships with the public.

ROLE PLAYS

- "In dealing with your complaint I want to make sure I uphold the code of ethics adopted by my organisation."

- "I believe the service you have received is not in line with the values set by the centre. On that basis, I will do all I can to put things right and keep you informed of progress at all times."

- "I will utilise the resources at my disposal to ensure the problem gets resolved quickly and competently."

- "In attempting to resolve this situation, I will endeavour to utilise all of the resources available to me here at the centre. This includes utilising the CCTV cameras to analyse where the missing person was last seen and also asking the security staff to immediately be deployed to safeguard the exits."

- "The reputation of the centre is very important, and we have strict guidelines in respect of how staff and members of the public should act. In this instance, it appears the guidelines have not been followed and I will now take appropriate action to deal with the situation."

- "My aim, whilst dealing with this situation, is to provide exceptional service at all times and I will achieve that by upholding the standards and ethics laid out by the centre."

Competency #12
Innovative And Open Minded

COMPETENCY #12 – INNOVATIVE AND OPEN MINDED

The final competency challenges the mindset of the candidate. It's extremely important that you can take an open-minded approach to police work. Not everything is straightforward and 'by the book'. There will always be problems which require an innovative and creative solution, and it's your job to come up with this! Furthermore, it's essential that you can have an open mind to new ways of working, and understand that continuous development is a necessity for any police officer.

Here's what you'll be required to demonstrate not only during the selection process, but also once you become a police officer:

> Being open to new perspectives, ideas and perceptions. Sharing ideas and suggestions with colleagues, with the aim of improving current police practice. Reflecting on their own working practice and how it can be improved. Adapting to changing circumstances and needs.

Let's now take a look at my suggested keywords, phrases and sentences for the core competency of INNOVATIVE AND OPEN MINDED. You will notice I have simply provided you with a list for the application form/interviews and a list for the role play scenarios. I believe each of these sentences will help you demonstrate the core competency of INNOVATIVE AND OPEN MINDED through what you write and say during the selection process.

APPLICATION FORM AND INTERVIEWS

- Whilst considering my options, I was open minded to all possibilities and suggestions that were being put forward by the team.

- Following the complaint from the customer, I put forward to my manager a number of suggested changes that would allow us to improve the overall customer service experience.

- Once the team task was complete, I recommended we all get together to discuss our performance with a view to seeing how we could improve for next time.

- During the project, an important member of the team went off due to sickness absence. We had to regroup and alter our plan due to the changing circumstances. We did this with positivity and enthusiasm.

- My manager made a number of suggestions that would change our working conditions and practices. I decided to embrace these changes as I believe change is positive and it can help to improve an organisation.

- Within my previous role I was never afraid to search for innovative ways to solve problems and I would openly share my ideas with other work colleagues and departments to obtain their view on my suggestions.

- At all times in previous roles I have been open minded whilst tackling problems, and I always sought innovative and creative solutions to the issues presented.

- I am someone who continually seeks different ways to improve and develop. In the last 12 months alone, I completed two development training courses which have had a positive impact on my work output and the level of service I provided for my employer.

ROLE PLAYS

- "I am open-minded to what might have occurred here. In order for me to gain a thorough understanding, please can you tell me exactly what has happened?"

- "Once the complaint is resolved satisfactorily, I will put forward a number of recommended changes to my manager which I believe will improve the operation of the centre."

- "Following this incident at the centre, I will get together with the rest of my team to look at ways we can prevent it from happening again."

- "I will maintain an open mind during this incident and be prepared to change my plan if the need arises."

- "If things need to change at the centre following this situation and what has happened to you, I will put forward the suggested changes to my line manager for review."

Sample Application Form Question & Answer (Competencies 7-12)

SAMPLE POLICE OFFICER APPLICATION FORM QUESTION & ANSWER (Competencies 7-12)

Once again, in this next short section of your guide, I am going to provide you with a sample police officer application form question and answer that is based on the previous 6 competencies. The answer provided is how I personally would respond to the question and is my attempt at matching the new core competencies that are relevant to the role of a police officer. As with the previous answer supplied, I have not utilised any of the keywords, phrases or sentences covered in the guide. Instead, I have created my own unique answer that I believe is a close match to the assessable competencies.

Q. Why have you applied for this post and what do you have to offer?

> I have applied for this post because, having studied the core competencies in detail, I believe I have the necessary skills, qualities and attributes to become a competent police officer. I thrive and perform to the best of my abilities within an organisation that has high standards and that sets itself important values. I want to work within an organisation that is held accountable by its stakeholders and that is required to constantly change and adapt to its customer's needs. I am an emotionally stable person who is able to think on my own initiative. Having previously worked as a team leader, I am someone who remains calm in difficult situations, who is able to motivate and inspire others whilst also delivering a great level of service. Although I am happy working on my own, I perform to the best of my abilities when working as part of a team, consistently delivering a high level of service. I can keep a cool head in times of stress and will always think things through carefully before making important decisions. I understand the police service requires its police officers to act responsibly at all times and act as positive role models for the organisation. I have the necessary experience, skillset and attributes to perform to a high level within this role.

Sample Assessment Centre Interview Question And Answer

SAMPLE ASSESSMENT CENTRE INTERVIEW QUESTION AND ANSWER

In this final short section of your guide, I will once again provide you with a sample police officer assessment centre interview question and answer based on the new core competencies. This is to show you how I personally would prepare my answers in line with the assessable core competencies. When preparing for the police officer assessment centre interview questions, don't forget to utilise the STAR technique for structuring your answers. Here is a breakdown of the STAR technique and how each element is used to provide solid, genuine answers to the following interview question:

Q. TELL ME ABOUT A TIME WHEN YOU DEMONSTRATED EMOTIONAL AWARENESS?

SITUATION

Whilst sitting in the work canteen one morning, I overheard a conversation between two work colleagues who were making inappropriate jokes and comments about another co-worker who was not present in the canteen.

TASK

Naturally, I was offended by the comments. Because the comments were against our organisation's values, I decided to act and ask them to stop. I felt it was my responsibility to ask them to stop and to also explain to them why their comments were not acceptable.

ACTION

I walked calmly over to the table and asked them to stop using the inappropriate language. One of the men looked up at me and told me in an angry voice to "Mind my own business!"

I remained calm and considered quickly my options. Although the situation had the potential to deteriorate further, I utilised a calm tone and an open body position and, once again, reiterated my position that I would like them to stop their comments. I then went on to explain how their language was offensive, but also the fact that it went against the organisation's values and code of ethics. I also explained that the person they were talking about was not there to defend themselves and that we should be all working together as a team, as opposed to making offensive comments.

RESULT

I could tell the man felt he had nowhere else to go with the conversation, as he was starting to look foolish amongst the other members of the workforce in the canteen. He eventually apologised and stated he understood how his comments were offensive and that he wouldn't use them again. Throughout the entire situation I considered my options and felt it was important to uphold the values and standards of the organisation. By remaining calm and in control at all times, I was able to reach a successful resolution.

A Few Final Words

I genuinely want you to succeed and achieve your goal of becoming a police officer. The only way you will succeed, however, is to focus on demonstrating the core competencies at every stage of the process. During your preparation for each stage of the selection process, block out all negativity in your life and work very hard to reach your goal.

If you feel you are lacking in any particular core competency, go out and get the experience. For example, if you have little or no experience of working with other people to provide an effective service, or if you have never worked within the community, go and volunteer in your local high street charity shop one day a week, or better still, go and volunteer at a homeless shelter!

Working in places such as these will not only give you invaluable experience and scenarios to draw upon during the selection process, but it will also give you a good insight into what goes on in your local community. To find out more about how you can volunteer in your local community, visit the following website:

www.do-it.org

In addition to the above website, I have also listed a small number of websites and resources that I feel may help you during your journey to becoming a police officer.

I wish you the very best of luck. Believe in your abilities, and you really can achieve anything you set your mind to.

Best wishes,

Richard McMunn

USEFUL RESOURCES

MY YOUTUBE CAREER ADVICE WEBSITE:

www.YouTube.com/CareerVidz

MY BESTSELLING POLICE OFFICER RECRUITMENT BOOK

www.PoliceOfficerRecruitment.co.uk

ATTEND A 1-DAY POLICE OFFICER TRAINING COURSE

www.PoliceCourse.co.uk

ATTEND A POLICE OFFICER ASSESSMENT CENTRE TRAINING COURSE

www.PoliceAssessmentCourse.co.uk

Printed in Great Britain
by Amazon